AROUND THE ROUND WORLD

Around the Round World

TRUE STORIES FOR BOYS AND GIRLS

by
RITA F. SNOWDEN

LONDON
THE EPWORTH PRESS

FIRST PUBLISHED IN 1962

© THE EPWORTH PRESS 1962

Book Steward
FRANK H. CUMBERS

SET IN MONOTYPE BASKERVILLE AND PRINTED IN
GREAT BRITAIN BY THE CAMELOT PRESS LTD
LONDON AND SOUTHAMPTON

To

MY FRIEND, B. H.

born story-teller, who remains
a child at heart

AUTHOR'S NOTE

I owe the facts contained in the story *Andre* to two friends, Mr and Mrs Trevor Shaw, who for a long time have been happy to work with Andre Massaki, Editor of *Sikama*.

Contents

Young Andrew

THE Cunninghams were the liveliest, happiest family. A sister and brother were already growing up and getting into scrapes when Andrew was born. Another brother and sister followed, so there were five of them, just a nice family for doing things.

Their home was in the lovely Irish city of Dublin, though both father and mother were Scottish. Father was a Professor at the great Trinity College, teaching young doctors how to be better doctors. But he was interested in lots of other things, chief of them, the Zoo. He loved animals, and Andrew and the others loved to go with him when he went to the Zoo. While he was busy there, they got to know all the keepers, and were allowed to go round with them, and see and do lots of things that ordinary boys and girls were not allowed.

Every year there were wonderful family holidays, when Father went fishing, and there were new places to explore.

Then, of course, came school, and Andrew went first to Mr Morley's, and then to Edinburgh Academy. More important, came the day for him to decide what he wanted to be in the world. Would he be a Professor like his father? No! Would he do things with animals? No! What would he do? Well, he hadn't made up his mind; but he was very fond of boats and the sea. Then one day, it all came plain. The important choice was made—and once made, Andrew never went back on it.

He was away at school—at the Academy in Edinburgh—when his father sent him a telegram. Andrew's heart fluttered as he tore it open; then he read the words: 'Would you like to go into the Navy?'

The thought of being with ships and the sea appealed to him very much. After he had thought about it for a little while, he sent the reply to his father—a very surprising reply: '*Yes, I should like to be an Admiral.*'

I think his father smiled when he got that. Certainly, young Andrew was aiming for the top! And why not?

Meanwhile, there were some other things to do, ordinary things that all boys have to do. There was so much that he didn't know. His maths were good, but his English was weak; his French was no better, and he couldn't abide Latin.

In time, Andrew passed on to another school, and, exactly eight days after his fourteenth birthday, to H.M.S. *Britannia*.

But he wasn't an Admiral yet. There were still many things to learn—dull things some of them, but now he was living with sixty-four other boys on a real ship.

Was it worth it? Oh, yes, of course. For in the end— *he became an Admiral*, and a very famous one too. It didn't happen all at once; one thing led to another; one hard task to its mastery. For his services, he earned a special medal, the 'D.S.O.', three times over. Best of all, he realized his dream and became what he wanted to be, and he was able to give great and important service to his country.

What do you want to be?

Somewhere today there is another little schoolboy who wants to be an Admiral. I wonder if that's you.

Somewhere there is a little girl who wants to be a Hospital Matron. And that's a great thing to be. But it's not possible all at once—first comes study, faithfulness in little things, a loving heart and great kindness.

It is always like that. You want to be an Admiral, a Matron, a Doctor, a Missionary? Of course you needn't wait till you leave school—you can start right away. You remember what Jesus said to His friends who wanted to be missionaries and do great things for Him: 'Ye shall be witnesses unto me both in Jerusalem [the place where they were], and in all Judæa [the next place], and in Samaria [the next place still], and unto the uttermost part of the earth' (Acts 1^8).

And you could begin like that, couldn't you?

John the Giraffe

I WONDER what John the Giraffe thought as he boarded the good ship *Illyric* in London. It was quite an adventurous trip for one so young, right from one side of the world to the other. John was only two years old, though he stood twelve feet high—the height of two tall men.

Fortunately, a good friend of his, a zoo supervisor called Mr Wood, was travelling on the same ship. John's neck was a little too awkward to fit into an ordinary bunk in a cabin, so a special place all his own was made for him up on deck. Of course, it was all very strange at first. He had to be loaded on to the ship by a crane, and the men at the docks were very interested in their curious passenger. One or twice when bareheaded men walked past John on the deck, the giraffe bent his head to snatch a good mouthful of hair off the top of their heads, and then they were more than merely interested.

John did not like the movement of the ship much when they got into the high seas, but as the days went by, he settled down and quite enjoyed the adventure. At every port the dockers were surprised, when they saw his curious head and neck peering from his place on the deck; and as they came slowly through the Panama Canal John got another mouthful of hair from an unwary docker on the bank.

One night in the tropics, when it was warm and calm enough to have a picture-show up on deck, John saw a lion. It was in the picture, of course, on the screen; but John didn't like it very much. Lions are old and dreaded enemies of giraffes.

The most exciting part of all was when the *Illyric*

pulled into Auckland, and the long voyage was over. Certainly it was an exciting time for the boys and girls who with others were there to welcome him. They gazed straight up at him in his place on the ship, and happily he gazed down at them.

Then the great business of getting him ashore began. It took some time. Great wire ropes had to be placed round his box, to make quite sure nothing would slip or break, and the box with John in it was lifted down on to the wharf.

Mr Wood, John's friend, was there to help and advise, of course, but it took a lot of others as well to get John in his box safely through the busy city streets, and out to his new home at the Zoo. Crews of workmen had to stand by, in case anything unexpected happened; John's long neck was inclined to come too near telephone wires, trolley-bus cables, and overhead live electric wires, so it was quite a business.

But at last, it was all safely managed, and the journey was over.

At the Zoo gates lots and lots of boys and girls who had heard the news of his coming were there to meet him. Only Jamuna the elephant seemed uninterested as she went on eating her grass; but to add to the welcome of the children, the parrots and pea-hens squawked, and the monkeys chattered.

John stayed in his box for a little while. By the late afternoon, he was ready to step out into his new yard, and stretch his legs. Everybody hopes that John the Giraffe will be very happy in his new home, half a world away from London, where he was born in Regent's Park Zoo. Here the children flock to see him.

But there is just one awkward thing about it—John is the only giraffe in all New Zealand, and there is a real fear that he might be lonely. It cost twelve hundred pounds to get John, and bring him all this way—and it is hoped that in three years time there will be enough money saved to bring another giraffe all the way from London to bear him company. Because, you see, even a giraffe can't be lastingly happy all by himself.

Nor can any one of us. That is the meaning of that very wise saying of one in the early days of the Christian Church: '*One Christian is no Christian.*'

We have to do things together!

Christmas in the Snows

THERE was good news for the Eskimos, Indians and half-breeds at Aklavik. The Bishop was coming—already his boat was expected at the little wharf. The Bishop was a man who loved boats and journeyed in them for thousands of dangerous miles.

For a long time, the good Bishop had been thinking of a piece of flat ground. Exactly at midnight, on the July night when he came into port, he saw it there in broad daylight. No, he was not dreaming—and you are not dreaming—Aklavik is one hundred and twenty miles north of the Arctic Circle, and there are times when it is light all night long.

Once, Aklavik had been very small, with few people to meet the Bishop when he came. Now it was different. So many people had come in their little boats between the ice-floes, and in sledges drawn by dogs that there was no place big enough to hold them all for worship.

That was what the Bishop's good news was about. 'We are going to build a big church,' he said, 'a cathedral where Eskimos and Indians and half-breeds, men and women and little children, shall all know welcome when they come to worship. We must make our cathedral as beautiful as ever we can.'

The people were glad and eagerly promised to help. Their gifts soon came pouring in, and on Sunday the offertory plates were heaped high with musk-rat skins.

Then a lovely thing happened. An Australian lady who had heard the Bishop preach wrote him a letter to say how interested she was in the building of the cathedral and asking if she might help. It wasn't that she was very rich, with much money to give, but she was an artist, and she volunteered to paint the altar-piece for the cathedral at Aklavik.

The Bishop was glad. He went at once to see some of the artist's work, and it was so beautiful that he knew that the altar-piece would be of the very best, and worthy of being offered to God.

At last the picture was finished, this beautiful picture of the Epiphany in the Snows. It shows clearly that God's love is for all people. The little Jesus and His mother are dressed in regal ermine—very soft fur only to be found in the North—and they are wearing Eskimo boots. Behind are two reindeer. On one side, where most pictures show the three wise men, offering their gold, frankincense and myrrh, stands an Indian, bringing a live beaver as a gift. Then, kneeling, is another man, with the best he has to give—a white Arctic fox-skin. Behind stands another with (what do you think?) two fine sledge dogs, one white, the other black, harnessed for service. Then on the other side of Mary kneels a man in the snow presenting two walrus tusks—the very best he has to give. Behind is an Eskimo woman, with a very kind face, and a baby of her own in her hood. They are all there to see the little Christ Child, and praise God for the most wonderful gift in all the world.

As the people of Aklavik meet for worship in their own cathedral, their colourful altar-piece helps them to realize that the Christ Child is present with them in the land of snows.

Three Little Ships

AN exciting letter was awaiting me on the breakfast table. It was from the Commander, asking me to have tea with him on Saturday at the house of the little Merchant of Aleppo. He told me how to find my way by train to a district of South-east London and, when I reached the house set in its fine garden, there waiting to receive me was the Commander. Before he led me inside to see the treasures, he told me the lovely story which I will now tell to you.

John Morden was the name of the Little Merchant. He was a goldsmith's son who lived in London, in the seventeenth century. Above everything, he loved ships, and whenever he was free, he made his way down to the River Thames to see the tall-masted ships sail up the river. 'Some day', he said to himself, 'when I am big, I'll get ships of my own, and sail away to strange lands, and buy beautiful things.'

This is just what he did. He got three little ships, with tall masts and rigging, and plenty of room below to stow beautiful things. With his heart full of dreams, he sailed away to the lands beside the blue Mediterranean, and found his way to Aleppo, a great trading-centre in Syria. Soon, he became known as the Little Merchant of Aleppo. He bought bales of silks, spices, and golden treasures, and stowed them in his three little ships, and sent them to London to be sold. He became rich, but after many years in Aleppo, he began to long for London. 'I know what I will do,' he said, when his three little ships had gone off, with orders to trade here and there on the way, 'I will make my way and wait here no longer;

home in London I shall receive the rich reward of their trading.'

But when at last the Little Merchant of Aleppo got to London, there was no sign of his ships and no news of them. At first, he was disappointed, and then very puzzled. Where could they be? Nobody could tell him. Days, and weeks, and months went by—and years.

The Little Merchant found himself poor, with all his treasures gone, and he had to think of ways to earn his bread. He hired himself to a gentleman as a servant.

Some time afterwards, while he was waiting on his master, he chanced to overhear a snatch of conversation that made his heart race. Three ships, it was said— three ships from the East—had arrived in the River Thames. After so long, he dared hardly hope; but when his work was done, he flung on his coat, grasped his hat, and ran for the Thames.

Could they be his, those three ships? Hardly daring to ask the question even under his breath, he ran on and on, past groups of men standing talking, till before him were the masts of three ships. *Yes, his three ships!*

Overcome with thankfulness, he fell at once on his knees, and made a promise to God that he would do something to help other merchants who might fall upon bad days. With the rich reward of his three ships' trading, he selected a piece of land by the river, at Black Heath. He then sought out the best architect of the day, his friend Christopher Wren, and took him to the place. He wanted his offering of thankfulness to be the very best that he could make it. Christopher Wren looked at the land beside the river, and set to work and drew some beautiful plans for a place that the Little Merchant of Aleppo meant to call Morden College.

There it stands to this day—still called Morden College —though it has nothing to do with lessons like most colleges. It is a beautiful home for aged merchants, with beautiful gardens, and a hospital and chapel. Added to all the hundreds who have lived there since the Little Merchant's day—thankful to God for his own thankful bequest—forty-five men live there today, including the Commander who invited me to tea. And it all started with the three little ships that came back!

Loud Cheers for George!

ONE moment the Lowe boys in their best clothes awaited the signal to set off on an outing; the next moment it was plain that there would be no outing that day.

Little George stood on the veranda, hands in trousers pockets. To fill in the time of waiting, his big brothers Arch and Jock began a friendly bout of boxing.

How it happened nobody knew, but next moment they had collided with George. Headlong over the veranda steps he crashed. When he woke up, he was lying, to his surprise, in the family sitting-room with his left arm hurting.

Soon the young doctor was leaning over George, and it was plain something would have to be done for him at once. He was whisked off to hospital, and Arch and Jock and the rest of the family went to bed very soberly that night.

They were even more sober at the end of the week—and at the end of the next eighteen months when the damaged arm had still not mended. Operation after operation was performed on it—the bone broken, set, re-broken, and set again. 'It looks pretty hopeless,' George overheard the doctor say, 'he'll never use that arm. I'm afraid he'll always be a bit of a cripple.'

George never forgot those words. Far from sinking back into self-pity, he decided they should never come true.

After schooldays he left the farm and his family to go away to college, and to university. He meant to be a teacher. His arm developed without muscle, but little did he know what adventures lay ahead of him.

George Lowe was at college when he had the chance to help some of his friends to recut a track that had become overgrown in a famous mountain district of the country. It was to be a holiday job—and they hoped, good fun. George was just twenty-one, and he had never been in the mountains before. More than that, it was his first holiday away from home, and he enjoyed every minute of it.

One day there, he fell into talk with a tall young man who had just arrived to go climbing in the mountains. 'What do you do when you are at home?' George asked.

'My father keeps a bee-farm,' he answered, 'and I help him.'

'My father runs a fruit-farm,' said George, 'with bee-keeping as a side-line. We get our queen bees from a chap in Auckland—someone called Hillary.'

'That's us,' said the tall young man, 'my name's Ed Hillary. Small world, isn't it?'

And from that meeting, their names were to be linked together in the great world.

When Ed Hillary was chosen to represent his country to try to climb the highest mountain in the world—Everest —George Lowe went with him. By this time, they had had a lot of practice together on mountains. But this was something really special. Everest would challenge all their powers. Those who would conquer that great peak would need great courage as well as skill and strength. Breathlessness, piercing headaches and vomiting would have to be overcome.

It took a long time to get ready. Hundreds helped. Special tents had to be made, special clothes, special boots. Oxygen-sets had to be tested for breathing high on the mountain, where the air was thin. Special ropes had to be got, and, together with special stores, carried high up the mountain. Lots of mountaineers had tried before—and failed. But this did not discourage the two young New Zealanders.

Ed Hillary with his Sherpa were the ones who got to the top; but without George Lowe it seems certain he would never have managed it. Colonel Hunt, the leader of the expedition, has told of the difficulty he had in finding a suitable way up over a certain steep face of the mountain. Snow fell daily, and the only way to get up was to hack great steps. Two of those who might have helped fell sick, and could do nothing.

It was George, with his Sherpa, who saw the job through. For four days, with falling snow in a freezing temperature, fifty degrees below zero, he stood out there hacking steps in the ice, with a wild hurricane wind lashing about the mountainside. It was a glorious effort—full of courage.

And so Ed Hillary and his Sherpa got to the top of Mount Everest!

But for no one in the climbing party was it a greater triumph than for George Lowe—*the boy who might have died of self-pity*.

A Bright Idea

HIGH up above the little town of Gisors stands a castle, very ancient and very strong. It has stone walls which seem to reach up, nearly into the clouds; and down inside, dark dungeons are cut right into the rock. Every one of its doors has an iron lock, made to turn only to the keeper's key. It is the kind of castle to strike fear into the hearts of those who have done wrong—and of the innocent too. For sometimes, by mistake, good people were locked up inside its dungeons in the old cruel days of long ago. Nowadays, visitors are allowed to go in and see the cell where one good prisoner was kept in captivity.

High up in the wall is a little square window cut into the stone—too high and too small to get through, but big enough to let in a little patch of sunlight during a few hours of each day. Otherwise, it is very dark and dismal. One day, after the good prisoner had been in the dungeon some time, he came across an old rusty nail wedged in between the big flat stones of the floor. It must have been unnoticed a long time, for it was rusty as well as bent. The captive held it between his thumb and finger. Then an idea came to him—a bright idea, in that dark place. He waited for the sun to travel across the sky until it made a little square patch of brightness upon his prison wall.

Taking up the rusty nail, he began to use the little square patch of sunlight, much as an artist would use his square of canvas, or as you might use a square of paper. But he had no colours—everything had to be done by patiently scratching on the stone with his rusty nail.

It took a long time to make a mark deep enough to show, but he kept on and on each day when the sun moved across the sky, and the little square patch of sunlight was upon his wall.

He was not carving his name, or thinking about himself at all. He was thinking about the One whom he loved most in all the word—the One who had called him to be His witness. (You know what a witness is—one who is called upon to speak up for someone, in a true way, no matter how hard it may be.) The good, brave prisoner was determined that nothing should spoil his witness to his beloved Lord and Master. So every day he did a little more—working with his rusty nail—until at long last, three little pictures were on his wall, just in that square where the sunlight fell.

The first was a little scratched-in picture of his Lord at Bethlehem—the little Son of God lying in the straw of the manger. The next one was of Him sharing His last supper with His disciples, to tell them some things He wanted them never to forget.

Last came a picture of the most sad, cruel day in all the world's story, when that same loved Master and Lord hung upon His cross high up on a hill outside a city wall.

By this time, the good, brave prisoner could do no more; his nail was worn right down, and all his own strength was used. But he was glad he had done his work. 'This is my witness,' he said, 'and some day, long after I am dead, people will come here, and will be led to think of the best and greatest in all the world, Jesus, my Lord and Master.'

Today, thousands of visitors go there, and as they look at the three little pictures they are grateful for the witness of the good, brave prisoner; but more than that, they seem to hear again the words of Jesus, said directly to them: '*Ye shall be my witnesses*' (Acts 1[8]). And they come away wondering and planning how best to do it.

The Children's Village

I WANT to take you to a village I know, high up on the side of a hill. The hill is in Switzerland, that beautiful, friendly little country full of green hills and tinkling cow-bells, lakes and mountains. There are lots of villages there, but this one is something very special. It is a children's village, and behind it is a wonderful story.

It all began as a dream in the mind of a Swiss doctor called Walter Corti. He was ill in hospital at the time. The war had just come to an end, and there were throngs of sad and sick and lost people in Europe—and throngs of sad and sick and lost children. Dr Corti thought about them every day. At last he wrote about them in a paper. 'Whatever we do for the grown-ups,' he said, 'something must be done for the children. They are the hope of the days to come. In this peaceful little country of Switzerland,' said he, 'long ago, children in need of love found a friend in that great man Pestalozzi, whose monument stands in a patch of grass beside a busy street in our city of Zürich. There he is shown bending down to listen to a little child. Let us listen to the needs of the children today—and carry on the same love that he showed them.'

People read Dr Corti's words, and their hearts were moved to build this beautiful village of winding streets and trees, and to call it Pestalozzi, after that great friend of needy children.

Of course, it took a lot of work. First, a piece of ground had to be found on which to build the village—a piece of ground where there would be lots of space for work and play, and plenty of fresh air, and friendly neighbours.

That was found above the village of Trogen, in the canton of Appenzell. It is an ideal place, where boys and girls from many countries can stay till they are fifteen or sixteen, and ready to go out into the world.

There they live today—children from Austria, Finland, France, Germany, Greece, Italy, Switzerland and Britain. The people in that part of Switzerland all speak German so the children learn to speak it too. That means that though they come from many countries, they can understand each other; and when they are together in work and play every day, it isn't so very hard. Some of the children can speak good English as well, as you will notice, if you are able to visit the village as I did a little while ago.

From Zürich we must take a train, for the village is sixty-five miles away. But we can't go all the way in one train; we have to change at a place called St Gallen, and get into a little mountain train that will climb up above the town, and puff its way in and out around the hillsides till we come to Trogen. Even then there is still a little farther to go—ten minutes' climb on our own good feet. As we climb, the view gets lovelier and the air sweeter. At last we shall see a fine stout post by the roadside, with the name of the village carved in wood. We have arrived.

It is such a high, happy place that my only fear is that some of you won't want to leave. There is so much to do—lessons, of course, and games, and music and handcrafts and painting and plays, and in the winter time when the snow is all around, glorious ski-ing. Oddly the British boys and girls have become the best at winter sports—I think because it is such fun, and they are so enthusiastic.

In each house lives a large family of about eighteen with a house-father and house-mother from their own country. They learn about their own countries and keep their birthdays, and Christmas, just as they would at home; but every day, as well, the different families do many things together.

That is the nicest thing about Pestalozzi Village. Each house has something to show the others, as each country in the world has something different to add to the life of all the others. The children of the village grow up to love and respect others—Austrians, Finns, French, German and Greek boys and girls, Italian, Swiss and British.

Two hundred have already gone out to work; some are stone-masons, some teachers, some sailors, nurses, others motor mechanics, and hairdressers. At Christmas-time, those who are not too far away love nothing better than to come home again; usually there are about sixty back for Christmas. You can imagine what a happy time they have, for it is a happy village, a happy community based on love and trust.

Before waving good-bye and puffing our way down again in the little mountain train, we may hear the children sing together one of their favourite songs. It is in German, but the opening words mean: '*You must always be brothers and sisters.*' That is how our Father, God, wants all His children in the world to live.

c

From Sunny Spain

ONCE, only a few in sunny Spain knew so much as the name of the young singer with the golden voice, Victoria de los Angelos. Now everybody knows her name, and millions of us have heard her sing. Wherever she goes, she is greeted with applause and armfuls of flowers.

'How did it all begin?' people ask, and they are told the story of the little girl who disturbed the students at their lessons. She lived with her father and mother in the fine city of Barcelona. Her father was the caretaker of the great University, and he had to keep the windows clean, the floors swept, and the courtyards and gardens tidy. He was happy in his work, but his happiness never found its way into song. He was all the more surprised when his little girl, as soon as she could babble, burst into childish song, and kept on singing.

As the students sat listening to their lectures, they could hear her singing—her pure, joyous child's voice rising from the courtyard below. Sometimes, when their work was dull, they forgot to listen to what their lecturers were telling them, and listened only to the little singer below. The students were happy enough, but the lecturers didn't like it. Something would have to be done about it, they said. So they gathered enough money to send the little singer to the great school of singing, called the Conservatory. As the days went by, her voice became ever more beautiful. From morning till night she sang, and those in the school of singing who taught her began to say that one day, if she kept on, she would have one of the most wonderful voices in the world. And she did keep on.

Sometimes, in the school of singing, she sang by herself; sometimes she sang with others in the choir. One day, when the choir was to sing, those who were to sing with her made a secret plan. They agreed to begin all together but when the song was well started, they would all suddenly stop. But when the full, rich singing of the choir came to an end it didn't mean the end of the song, for *one voice went on singing, just the same*.

What would happen to your youth choir if everybody suddenly stopped—would you be found doing your best?

And what would happen in your youth club, if everybody else stopped away one night—would you still be there?

What would happen in your church, your school, your town, if everybody suddenly left off being Christian—could you still be counted on?

It was this that Paul had in mind when he wrote to his Christian friends in the first century: 'Be ye stedfast, unmoveable, always' (1 Corinthians 15[58]).

On the Top of the Mountain

THE warm blue seas fringed with white surf lapped the sands of beautiful Hawaii. People from many countries paddled their outrigger canoes or swam. It was holiday time for the children, and for some of the grown-ups too. The rest were hard at work—in the shops and the houses, cutting the tall green sugar-cane and gathering in the golden, juicy pineapples.

Soon the children were hard at work, too—happy work, at which they laughed and sang, work of their own choosing.

High above the streets of Honolulu, the city by the sea, rose a wonderful mountain called old Punchbowl. Once it had been a live volcano, but now it was extinct, and everybody loved old Punchbowl.

At Easter-time each year a great white cross, forty feet high—as high as seven men—was erected up there. A wonderful sight it was—in the daytime clear against the sky, at night illuminated by strong, white searchlights.

From Good Friday till Easter Sunday it stood on the mountain-top. And year by year on Easter Sunday morning—the morning when, long ago, Jesus rose from the dead—thousands made their way to the mountain-top for a wonderful service. Just as the sun rose out of the sea surrounding their island, they listened to the reading from the New Testament, and sang their Easter hymns.

But on that windy mountain-top it was hard for the cross to keep erect, and people began to wonder what would have to be done.

Then a wonderful idea came to one of them, Mr Arthur

Powlison. He gathered the children together and told them his plan.

Soon they were hard at work. Altogether there were five thousand of them—boys and girls whose parents had been born in Korea, China, Japan, America, Portugal, England, New Zealand, Australia and other countries.

Soon, all the children were looking everywhere for stones—little ones, big ones—in their own yards and gardens, in the stream beds, up on the hillsides. For a whole week they kept at it, until they had gathered a huge heap.

How were they to get the stones to the top of the mountain? That problem didn't delay them for long. And the way they did it was the most exciting and wonderful part of all.

Starting from the pile at the bottom they made a living chain—standing hand to hand along the street, across a park, up and up, a mile and a half, right to the top of the mountain. Beginning with the boy and girl closest to the pile, they passed them one at a time, from hand to hand, up and up. With the children from many countries working together the task was soon done; every single stone was carried to the top of the mountain to form a support to steady the cross on its lofty hill.

So the great cross stands high and firm today. Easter by Easter, the people of Hawaii remember not only the triumph of Jesu's love, but also the triumph of human love!

Jimmy, the Young Inventor

WHEN the sun went down, and it was time to come indoors and light the lamp, little Jimmy Price loved to listen to the stories his father and mother told. There were no electric lights in Jimmy's home—only the lamp, and candles for when story-time was over, and the little boy had to find his way up to bed. In the velvety darkness, the yellow tongue of his tiny candle made a very small light. Sometimes, it threw queer shadows on the un-lighted parts of the passage as Jimmy went along. Some-times even in the corners of his room when he had left his clothes over the end of the bed, the shadows looked like strange creatures out of his story-books, or the Land of Make Believe.

At bed-time, Jimmy's head was full of stories—stories of great men, and the wonderful things they did. He hoped one day to be able to do wonderful things himself. He wanted to be an inventor. But never did it enter his dreams that he would be associated with one of the world's greatest inventors. But that is what happened. Jimmy had his share in making one of the most wonderful things —a lamp. Unlike the one his mother lighted, and carried to the table each night before story-time, it needed no oil and no wick to make it burn.

At first, when Jimmy Price walked into the workshop of Mr Edison, that great inventor hardly noticed him, he was so intent on what he was doing. Then he looked up. 'What do you want, sonny?' he asked.

'Please, I want to be an inventor,' said Jimmy. 'Can I come and help you, and learn to do things?'

Mr Edison was quiet for a few moments; then he said: 'Yes, I think you may.'

Jimmy could hardly believe his good fortune.

But the next thing was where was he going to live.

'In the workshop,' said Jimmy.' 'It looks a very nice workshop.'

And where was he going to sleep, Mr Edison wanted to know. The answer was the same: 'In the workshop.' He would be all right there, he felt sure, under one of the benches. He was so eager to be an inventor.

So it came about that Jimmy Price became Mr Edison's assistant.

At this time the great inventor was busy trying to make a new light. He had tried and tried and after nine thousand attempts there was still something not quite right. Mr Edison was not one to give up; so he tried again, and at last it looked as if it would be successful. This time he had used a carbon filament—the little thread-like thing inside the glass bulb, that was to carry the electricity, and give light.

Then a dreadful accident took place. It was Jimmy's fault, and he couldn't think how it happened; but one moment the precious new lamp was whole in his hands, and the next it lay smashed on the ground at his feet. He must have tripped in his excitement and haste to test the new lamp.

And now it was broken—smashed to atoms.

Mr Edison could have flown into a rage and sent Jimmy from his workshop for ever. But he wasn't that sort of man. He realized that it was nothing but an accident and so, without a word, the great inventor began all over again.

This time, when the new lamp was finished, Mr Edison did another very wonderful thing—he asked Jimmy to carry it to where he wanted it. 'Careful!' was the only word he said. Jimmy, his tears long forgotten, came out from behind the door of the workshop, and carried the new lamp safely upstairs; and when it was connected, it lit up!

To Jimmy, it seemed a truly wonderful thing—a lamp without oil or wick. But it was nothing like so wonderful as the words that his master, Mr Edison, said: '*That's one thing about our mistakes, Jimmy: they don't need to be permanent.*'

In the Little Straw-thatched House

OLD Kim Ich-Tong lived in a village in an out-of-the-way part of Korea. His home was a little straw-thatched house with dried mud walls, and the chimney went under the floor, to keep it warm at night. At one end of the kitchen was a great bowl for cooking rice. Rice was very important to farmers like Kim Ich-Tong. All day he worked hard on the land, and when he came home at night he was hungry.

Old Kim Ich-Tong knew nothing of the outside world, until one day he had to go to Pusan, the great city. There, to his surprise, he saw things he had never seen before. There were great houses—not a bit like his own little straw-thatched house—streets of them all close together. People filled the streets, walking, talking, buying and selling. Every moment was full of wonder to the eyes of old Kim Ich-Tong. At night, when he returned to the house where he was staying, the greatest wonder of all awaited him.

He did not say anything to anyone, but he made up his mind that when he went home he would spring a surprise on his farmer friends, who had never been to the far-away city of Pusan.

Old Kim Ich-Tong could hardly wait. For the greatest wonder to him in that great city was a strange light—an electric light—that came on when a little switch on the wall was pressed. From the ceiling above his head hung a cord, and at the end of it was a little glass bulb where the light lived when he pressed the switch. It was all a great wonder, and the old farmer made up his mind to get such a light for his own little straw-thatched house.

So on the next day, he went out into the busy street with its throngs of people, and pushed his way to a shop where such things were shown for sale. He bought first some cord, and the shop-man rolled it into a tiny coil; then he bought a switch for the wall; and last of all, a glass bulb—nicely packed, to keep it from breaking—for the little new light to live in.

Excited at his plan, old Kim Ich-Tong paid over his hard-earned money and left the shop with his parcels.

Soon, it was time to go home.

It was a long way, and he was tired when he reached the village and his little straw-thatched house. He laid his parcels down safely, and slept.

First thing next morning he poked a hole into his ceiling, and fixed the cord; next he fixed on the clear glass bulb, just above his head, and he put the switch into the wall.

Then, with great excitement, he went out to see his friends, and invited them to come to his house. They were only too ready to come. 'But do not come till it is dark tonight,' said the old man in his friendly village way.

At the proper time, they all came, slipping off their plaited-straw shoes at the door of the little straw-thatched house. In they came, the men wearing their hats, as was the custom, the women without hats. Together with the boys and girls who had come, too, they squatted comfortably on the clean, smooth oiled-paper floor—and waited.

At the right moment, when darkness had properly come, old Kim Ich-Tong told of his surprise, and rose and snicked down the switch. Do you know what happened? *Nothing—exactly nothing!* You have guessed why. Yes, poor Kim Ich-Tong had got all the parts right for his new light—but he hadn't got the power. Wasn't it a pity?

That is like some people: they have all the parts of being a Christian right—going to church, and reading the Bible, and singing hymns—but they haven't the power of Jesus—the power of Love—to make all these things work. Jesus says to us, '*Ye are the light of the world*' (Matthew 5¹⁴), *but the power is His! He must give us that.*

Exploring Together

PHILIP and Jane had been looking forward to the holidays for a long time. They were to go south to the great city of Melbourne, to stay with Uncle John and Auntie Janet. They had never been in Melbourne before, and there were lots of things to see—fine streets and shops, great buildings higher than any they had seen, and trees and gardens.

But the thing they liked best was something they discovered all by themselves—a bronze memorial showing a man with a little donkey. The little donkey, with his long ears up, and his head down, was carrying a heavy load—a sick, wounded man.

'I know who it is,' said Jane, 'we had about him in Sunday-school. You know, the man who came down the road where the robbers were. What was his name?'

'I know,' said Philip, 'we had about him, too. He hasn't got a name; he's just called the Good Samaritan. But I think this must be different, because look, here are some words.' And Philip read the words on the memorial: 'Private John Simpson, 3rd Field Ambulance, A.I.F.' Then drawing breath, he went on: 'After landing at Gallipoli, Simpson, with his little donkey, worked alone day and night taking water to the front line, and carrying the wounded back to the dressing-station. He and his little donkey were killed by a shrapnel on 19/5/15. Simpson was mentioned in despatches.'

Said Jane: 'I'm sorry he died; such a strong, kind man.'

That night, when they got back from their exploration in the great city, they told Uncle John about the strong, kind man with the little donkey, and how Jane thought first that he was the Good Samaritan.

'Well, in a way, he was,' said Uncle, 'because he did the same kind of things that the Good Samaritan did. Only it wasn't robbers on the road from Jerusalem to Jericho that had knocked this man out—it was war. But the results were much the same. And it took the same kind of courage to lift a badly wounded man on to his donkey, and holding him, to walk all along the way to safety. You know how Jesus spoke of the Good Samaritan: He said, "*He had compassion on him*". "Compassion" is a word we don't often use these days,' said Uncle, 'but it is a good word that means all the good things we've been saying about the Good Samaritan—pity and strong kindness and helpfulness.'

'Philip read the words about the man with the little donkey,' said Jane. 'It told his name, and said about his compassion'—Jane stumbled over the word, but she knew what it meant now—'it told about him taking water to the thirsty, and bringing the wounded man back.'

'That's right,' said Uncle, 'and he did it more than once. Again and again he made the journey.'

'How brave he must have been,' said Jane.

'Yes, he was,' said Uncle, 'and kind and helpful. And anybody can be like him—anybody that is, who shows compassion—and everybody gets some chances.'

'Even boys and girls?' queried Philip.

'Yes, even boys and girls,' said Uncle.

Young Tom

TEN paces inside Wesley's Chapel, London, is a plaque on the wall to bring to our minds the story of young Tom Protheroe.

Tom lived in London, and he was a very naughty boy. From the time he opened his eyes in the morning, till he closed them at night, he was up to some sort of mischief. If a street-stall man chanced to drop an orange he was serving, Tom would be sure to snatch it up as it rolled, and make off with it. If a bunch of boys decided to tie a tin-can to a stray dog's tail, Tom would be sure to have a share in it.

No wonder the teachers at Radnor Street Sunday School held their breath when Tom turned up. Some of his mates brought him along. Sunday by Sunday, they were sent to Sunday-school by their parents, wearing their best clothes and shoes. But Tom was different. Nobody at home cared where he went on Sundays, or what he wore. Sometimes he was shabby, sometimes early, sometimes late—and always he was up to some mischief.

During the singing he would lay tin-tacks on the seat in front; during prayer-time he would giggle or make others giggle. In class, he was just as bad, until the teacher despaired of ever teaching anything she had prepared, and all because of Tom.

At last, one Sunday afternoon, Mr John Wild Gabriel, the superintendent, felt he must do something he never wanted to do—expel Tom. Sad at heart, he called Tom up to his desk. He had tried every way to keep order in the Sunday-school but all seemed wasted on Tom. He

would not sing, he would not pray, he would not listen—
all he cared about was mischief. He would have to be
expelled.

Then suddenly, from beside the desk, one of the lady
teachers spoke up: 'Oh, please, don't do that, Mr Gabriel.
I will take Tom.'

'But he will upset your class,' warned the sad superintendent, 'as he has upset every other class he has been in.
Surely it would be better to let him go.'

Still the lady teacher persisted, and finally, it was
agreed that Tom should go into her class.

Young Tom, she knew, had no one at home who really
cared for him. So from the very start she set out, in all
the ways she could, to show him that she was interested
in him. She remembered his birthday when it came round.
In many small ways, she kept him busy, and in time she
won his trust and love. Now it was Tom who kept the
class in good order. There was nothing that Tom would
not do for his teacher.

But outside Sunday-school, it was not quite so easy.
Mischief still lurked in his busy brain. On Sunday nights,
with Thomas Thorpe his mate, young Tom loved to sit
up in the gallery in Wesley's Chapel. One night, bent
on mischief, he carried into church in his pocket a bird
that he meant to release as soon as 'the old parson' started
his sermon.

But that bird was never released. For standing to
announce his text, the preacher pointed straight at Tom
up in the gallery, and said: 'Thou art the lad!'

'He's spotted us,' whispered Tom. And the poor bird
stayed where it was for the rest of the time whilst the
preacher went on.

Years passed.

Eventually, both boys became Christians, and knelt at
the Communion rail in Wesley's Chapel, where so many
have offered their young lives to a new Master.

From the start Tom Protheroe, with his mate, was all

eagerness to help. Tom bought himself some books. It was only a few pence he could spare, but soon he was up at five o'clock every morning reading. How well he learned is seen in the fact that he became a local preacher.

His next great longing was to go to China. But the Church would not accept him. Undaunted, Tom offered his services to the China Inland Mission, but they too rejected him.

Disappointed, but still determined, Tom thought the matter over, and set off to earn some money. His pay was very little, and it took a long time to save much, but as soon as he had money in his pocket he went back to the Mission. 'I do not need any money,' said he, 'and I will work my own passage on the ship to China!'

How could they refuse such a missionary?

And to China he went. And a wonderful missionary he became. He learnt the language, and customs; he preached to the people, and built churches and schools, and did many exciting and wonderful things.

And always, when he returned to London, he went back to visit his old Sunday-school where, though he had been so long a naughty boy, *he learned the power of Love*.

Catching!

Do you catch things—things like mumps and measles?
Once, there was a little girl who caught an appetite.
That was an odd thing to catch, wasn't it? And she
was a Princess, too.

Her name was Marie Louise—Princess Marie Louise of
Bulgaria. She was only five. For some reason, she lost
her appetite. Everybody began to be very troubled about
it, and no wonder; a little girl five years old, who wouldn't
eat, was cause for worry. Daily she got thinner and
thinner. The Royal Doctor thought and thought what
could be the matter—and he couldn't find out. The
Royal Cook thought and thought what he could make,
and he couldn't prepare anything that would tempt the
little Princess.

Then one day her father, King Boris, hit upon a fine
idea. He sent to the State school for eight little children.
Their parents were so poor that they were always
hungry, when they got up and even when they had
eaten their breakfasts. They set off for school at the
proper time, but as their lessons continued, the little
niggling hunger within them grew into a big hunger.
At dinner-time they ate all that their parents could get for
them, but when they rose from the table the big hunger
had only been replaced by a little hunger. It was still
there and it lasted on till bed-time.

So they were glad to take part in the King's plan and to
go to the palace to eat with the Princess, Marie Louise.

At first, they couldn't believe it. The Royal table with
eight new little seats drawn up to it, was set with all the
things that boys and girls most love, ices and fruits and

D

chocolate cakes, and lovely puddings, and jellies, and ever so many more things. It made such a pretty sight, the eyes of the little poor children nearly popped out. They were invited to eat as much as they liked. And they did. Never had anything of the kind happened to them before; it was wonderful. But the little Princess left everything before her untouched.

Next day, as the King had planned, the children came again, and the table was spread again just as abundantly. By this time the poor children didn't need any urging to eat. The Princess could hardly take her eyes off them —and before the meal was ended, when they laughed, she laughed. But still she didn't eat.

Next day, the children came again. By this time they not only enjoyed their meal, and laughed, but sang as well. And without thinking of it, the Princess joined in —not in the eating, but in the laughter and song.

So it went on every day—each day better than the last. On the fifth day the Princess found herself not only joining in the joy of the children, but for the first time in many weeks she put some of the good things on her plate. When the news was passed to the King, he was very hopeful, and so was the King's Doctor, and the King's Cook.

On the sixth day—never to be forgotten—the Princess Marie Louise caught her appetite, and by the end of the week all was well.

It is amazing what boys and girls catch. Some catch only bad things—bad habits, bad words—which is a pity. Some catch good things—courage, and kindness— and this is wonderful.

Those who met the first friends of Jesus noticed how they caught things. They said: These young men are changed—they have courage and joy they never had before: 'They took knowledge of them, that they had been with Jesus' (Acts 4¹³).

And that still happens.

The Harvest Bell

LONG ago, in little Gross-la-witz, in northern Germany,
the people planned to get a new bell for their church.
They were simple people, and poor; but there was no
doubt that they needed a new bell. Every Sunday some
of them came late for church. Even when the weather
was fine, sunny and calm, the sound of the bell in their
church tower was so soft that they couldn't hear it at a
distance, and the old who were a little deaf, couldn't hear
it at all.

'What we need', said one of them, 'is a new bell.'

'Yes,' they all agreed, 'what we need is a new bell.
But how can we pay for it? A bell with a loud pleasant
voice that would bring us all to church would cost a great
deal.'

For a long time no one could think how they could buy
the new bell. Then something unexpected happened.
Sunday by Sunday, on his way to church, the schoolmaster had to pass by an old wall. It had stood for so
long that the winds had blown dust into its crevices;
and the sun and the rain had beaten upon it. It was a
lovely old wall, and the schoolmaster took very special
notice of it.

For there, one morning, he found growing in a deep
crevice, blessed by the sun and rain, a strong stalk of
corn. His first thought was that a bird had dropped
the seed there, and then he thought of the church
bell.

Week by week, as he went by, changes were noticeable.
At first the stalk was slender and green. By and by, it
began to fill out; and at last, it ripened into a lovely

golden colour. All the time the schoolmaster watched it carefully.

When it was time to harvest it, he gathered it and took it home. He shook out the golden seed, and laid it away in a safe, dry place.

When the time for planting came, he took it out, and carefully planted it in his tiny garden. In time it came up; in time it grew golden, and he was able to gather it again. This time he had a lot more. Once again he planted it and soon he had to call in his neighbours to help, for his own tiny garden wasn't big enough. Year by year they planted, and gathered, and planted and gathered—for eight years! At the end of that time they had a large harvest, and they were able to sell it.

With the money they got for their corn, they bought— what do you think?—yes, a bell for their church—a bell with a strong, pleasant voice that could be heard anywhere.

On the bell itself, before it was hung in the little church tower, they had engraved a six-eared stalk of corn—and the date: October the 15th, 1729.

Ever since, Sunday by Sunday, and especially at harvest-time, the good people of Gross-la-witz ring their bell joyfully, and gather to thank God, who out of His great care for us, gives the harvest.

Yondi

LONG, long ago—before any white people were in the great country of Australia—there were many more black aboriginal people there, black fathers and mothers and little black children. They had no towns, and no schools or books, but at night time they used to gather round the camp fire to tell stories under the starry sky.

One of the favourite stories was about Yondi, and it never failed to fascinate the girls and boys who heard it. It told of the beginning of the boomerang, the native weapon fashioned of wood curved at a clever angle. (A boomerang appears flattish, and is rounded on one side with one sharp edge. There are two kinds—one for fighting enemies, that drops where it is thrown; the other—by far the more interesting—the returning boomerang, used for hunting. It is from about twelve to thirty inches long, and weighs upwards of twelve ounces. It takes a clever father to make one, and a very clever father to throw one—so that when the boomerang is thrown at a wild animal needed for food, it will hit the target and come back to the thrower.)

In the lives of the boys and girls who listened to the story, a boomerang was one of the most important things in the world. No wonder they were fascinated by the story of Yondi. It was the story of how the sky was lifted, away back in the Dream Time—the time when nothing was as it is now.

Yondi was a warrior and one day he found a flat stick in a magic pool. He took a firm hold of the stick, and with it, set out to raise the sky. For the sky—the story said —was close to the ground in those times, and every man and beast crawled, and little low shrubs clothed the ground. With his great strength, Yondi put his stick under the low sky, and began to heave it up. Some of the water of the magic pool flew up into the heavens as he did it, and that gave the first rain as it fell back to the earth.

The stunted, shrubby trees then began to grow, and the birds to fly—wings breaking from their sides as they went. The kangaroo stood up on his hind legs to see the new wonder—and he has been standing that way, the story says, ever since. The emu stretched his neck so much to see, and ran so fast, that he has stayed that way ever since. Only the animals that were fast asleep when all this happened, now creep and crawl.

When Yondi took away the flat stick that he had used to prop up the great weight of the sky, he found that it had become bent—*and in his hand was the first boomerang*. Nobody knows for sure why it is called that: but every time Yondi threw it away, it returned to him, and the best boomerangs, properly thrown, have been doing that ever since.

No wonder the little black aboriginal children chuckled with delight as the story was told beside the camp-fire, under the great sky full of stars.

But boomerangs are not the only things that come back when they are thrown—angry words have a way of doing that, haven't they? Kind words and loving deeds come back, too. Long ago Jesus said: '*The measure you deal out to others will be dealt back to yourselves*' (Luke 6[38], Moffatt). Isn't that what He meant?

White Cottage

NOBODY in all London could remember such a fuss—and all about an old apple-woman! She was a cunning old apple-woman.

The place she had picked for her stall was in Hyde Park. At first nobody took much notice of her, but soon the old apple-woman—Ann Hicks—had an idea. As usual, when an idea danced into her old brain, she took pen and paper and wrote a letter. Then she folded it, and sent it off to somebody important—the Commissioner of Woods and Forests, who took care of Hyde Park. 'People who don't want to buy my apples might like to buy something else,' said she cleverly. 'Is it all right for me to sell them toothsome toffees and buns?'

'Certainly,' came the reply.

But it wasn't long before the cunning old apple-woman had another idea—and of course, wrote another letter. 'It's back-aching work moving all my goods in and out: I would like to be able to lock them up at night.'

'Of course, Mrs Hicks,' came the reply. 'It must be hard work, as you say.'

So the cunning old apple-woman had the little lock-up built, with a good, sturdy key.

But it wasn't long before she had another idea. 'The people who buy my buns', she wrote this time, 'would like to buy drinks of ginger-beer. They get so thirsty. Is that all right?'

'Why, to be sure,' came the reply; 'they must get thirsty.'

But that was not the end of it. The ginger-beer bottles

stood so tall on the shelf, they were awkward. 'I'd like to raise the roof of my little lock-up,' wrote the old apple-woman.

'By all means,' came the reply.

And while the workmen were at it, she had it raised nearly as high as herself—five feet!

Nor was that the end of the ideas that danced into her lively old mind. 'The roof isn't very waterproof,' she wrote, 'the rain comes in, and spoils my goods when there's a storm. Can I put up a few tiles?'

The reply came. But when the workmen arrived, she said to them: 'A roof is good, but why not a nice little chimney as well—and while you are here with your tools, why not a nice little window?'

So the cunning ideas of old Ann Hicks took shape—'here a little and there a little'.

But she had not yet come to the end. She wrote that cheeky boys bothered her. Could she put up a little wooden fence to keep them back?

When permission was given, she said to herself: 'But what a pity to have it so near the house; if I pushed it back I could plant flowers inside it.' And that is what she did.

Having done so much, she thought it would be an idea to give the little place a name. It hardly seemed worth writing a letter about that—so she didn't bother this time: she merely put up a name: 'White Cottage'. For 'here a little, and there a little' the cunning old apple-woman had set herself up in a comfortable little house, where no house should be at all—with a key to its lock-up door, a tiled roof, chimney and window, and fence and garden! And there, cheekily defying all who came, it stood for many a day at the eastern end of the Serpentine in Hyde Park.

Then one day, news went out that there was to be a Great Exhibition—and it was to be in Hyde Park. A committee of clever people set out to see where was the best place in the Park to put it. Among them was the Commissioner of Woods and Forests!

To their amazement, there before them stood a little house—'White Cottage'—where no cottage should be at all, rent free, in the public park. At once they told old Ann Hicks she had no right to be there—and that if she didn't move there'd be trouble. She protested that she had asked permission; but she had worded her letters so carefully and cunningly, of course, that no one had any idea what she was up to. And always when she had been granted permission, she had taken a little more.

Some said she should be allowed to stay, to sell apples and toffees and bottles of ginger-beer in the Park, but most said she had no business there at all. The matter got into the London newspapers; some said this, and some said that. In the end, it was taken to Parliament to settle. Of course, it was no good—old Ann Hicks had to move out of the Park. But she fought for her cunning ideas to the very last apple.

People were amazed; how, they asked, had such a thing ever happened? But it was plain enough—'here a little, and there a little' (Isaiah 28[10]).

In this amazing world, most wrong things are like that —they don't appear all at once. Those of us who love fair things and honest have to see that they are stopped before they grow into something settled.

Four Little Books

'What's the matter? What are you doing?' asked Pak's wife, summoning up all her courage, for she feared him when his face was flushed. Pak was known in the market-place of Chungju, as the worst drinking, fighting, gambling man in that part of Korea. Many besides his wife feared him.

'We are going to move to the Kongnim monastery to farm there with the Buddhists,' said Pak. 'It's no use trying here, where all my money goes. I've a promise of land. Come on, pack, pack, pack!'

Hastily they gathered their few things—cooking pots, coverings and clothes, and together they set off over the mountains.

At last they came to the place where Pak planned to farm. At first, he worked hard—sometimes up to his knees in his rice-pond, where the ice still floated. All promised well, until Pak carried his beans and lentils into the market. Then, just as on the other side of the mountains, he came staggering back, with nothing left of his pay.

'This Buddhist religion is as hopeless as my old Confucianism' he declared. 'All it says is, "Be good, be good, be good!" But it gives no power to be good. We have gained nothing by coming over the mountains!'

It was quite true, and things did not improve until one day, Pak came upon a bright-faced traveller in the market-place. He had a little donkey, and a bag of books, and Pak watched him go from inn to inn, from stall to stall. 'What books are those you carry on your little donkey?' asked Pak.

The traveller replied: 'These are books of Glad Tidings. They tell of God, who gives power to battle against bad things, and to find happiness.'

Pak looked round to see if anyone was watching him. Then he drew from his bag some little coins—eight *sen* —enough for four of the little books.

That night, eager to read them, Pak got home earlier than usual. His wife was surprised to see him and set to work at once to prepare the meal. Then she poured oil into a saucer, placed in it a twist of cotton wick, lighted it, and sat down. Holding one of his little books to the light, Pak began to read aloud. The more he read as they sat in their simple home, the more interested he became.

Night after night, when work was done he hurried home.

At last, all four little books were finished—the Gospels of Matthew, Mark, Luke and John.

While Pak was wondering what to do next, he met another traveller. He was a teacher and another happy man and when he was invited, he taught Pak and his wife and neighbours the meaning of what was written in the four little books.

One night he said, his face brighter than ever, 'I have good news for you. I have taught you all I know, but on the third night of the new month, a missionary will pass this way. Would you like him to stop as he passes?'

'Thank you,' said Pak, excited, 'we should like that very much.'

On the third night of the new month, with lighted torches made of thin, dry sticks tied in bundles, they all went down to meet the passing missionary. He was surprised when he saw the people waiting. Happily, they walked together past the tall gateway and on and up till they came to Pak's little house.

Every spring and autumn after that, when the missionary passed, he stopped to share more with the welcoming people. Pak went on reading his little books, over and over, and every time he found something in them he had never found before—about God, and the power to battle against bad things, and to replace them with God's happiness.

And in time, Pak himself became the leader and friend of all the farming people in that place. So great was the change in him, that when he travelled over the mountains, the people who had known him when he lived there, at first, didn't know him—*for now his face shone, too.*

Andre

ANDRE's black face shone with the pride of a little African brother, as he looked at Baby Sister on Mother's back, as she sat preparing the midday meal outside their home.

Then the thing that he would never forget happened. He could not fully understand it all at once, he was too little. It had to do with Aunt, and Mother, and the old Chief. Into their quiet family circle the guards had come tramping, and with rough words had hounded off Andre, Mother and Baby Sister to the house of the Chief.

'Take this woman', the Chief had ordered, blaming Mother for things she had not done, 'and give her a hundred lashes of the whip!' Andre couldn't believe his ears, and the next minute, the first of the four guards armed with whips, moved to carry out their Chief's bidding. With all his little strength of seven years, Andre tried to defend Baby Sister and Mother. But it was no use. Under the cruel lashings, Mother toppled, and they fell senseless to the ground. The instant Andre knew that his little sister was dead, he cried out his revenge: 'You wait! You wait!'

Mother managed somehow to drag herself away from the place of whipping. In a few days, full of fear that the guards would do something dreadful to Andre, she sent him away to a distant village. She hated to let him go, but he was to stay with a kind Christian relation who she believed would take care of him.

The relation got the little boy into a Mission School. It was new and wonderful for Andre, and he was happy till news reached him that his mother had died. Then all the bitterness sown in his heart on that terrible morning, rose again: 'You wait!' he cried. 'Wait till I'm grown up. I'll get my revenge!'

But as the years passed, and Andre grew up, something more wonderful happened. One day, news reached him that the very guard who had lashed to death those he loved, was come to live in the place where he was now living. At the news his heart thumped wildly. He could hold his secret hate no longer. His kind relation, whom he had learned to call 'Uncle', guessed that something was wrong. All the boyish joy in his eyes had given place to a hard look. At last, Andre told him about the guard.

'And what are you going to do?' asked Uncle.

'Avenge my loved ones,' said Andre.

But next moment—lowering his voice till it was very soft—Uncle asked a further question: 'Is it true that you are a Christian?'

'Yes,' replied Andre, 'I am a Christian now.'

'Then,' said Uncle, very gently, 'are you going to forget what is in the Bible: "Avenge not yourselves . . . vengeance is mine, I will repay, saith the Lord"?'

Andre's eyes filled with anger: 'I must do it! I must do it!' he cried. But Uncle's words were beginning to tell. 'Has not God forgiven you?' he asked, 'Revenge is not the way of a Christian. You must forgive.'

Andre bent his head.

For many days he kept off the streets, lest he should meet the guard who had come to live near. The old pagan revenge still rose to his mind when he thought of him; but gradually a new power laid hold of his heart. One day, when he was out with friends, the guard he had feared to meet joined them. Andre was not sure the guard even knew who he was; that morning of lashing was so long past. Andre excused himself, and went on alone. He wanted to think; he wanted to pray—it was not easy.

At last, when he felt himself strong enough, he sent

word to the guard to come to his own house. When the guard learned who Andre was, fear struck his heart. He felt sure of only one thing—Andre had trapped him, and was was about to take his revenge.

But he was wrong—gloriously wrong. Instead, Andre for the first time, with all his heart, had learned to pray the Lord's Prayer: 'Forgive us, as we forgive.'

Today, Andre has little boys and girls of his own; and a very dear friend, as close to him as a brother, is the guard, who, forgiven, has become a Christian, too. *So the sad story has a happy ending.*

Little Carl

LITTLE Carl Linné loved the flowers that grew in his father's garden. His father was a poor preacher, in the village of Rashult, away in Sweden. But little Carl never felt poor. Around his father's door bloomed wild flowers without number, and there were others to be sought and found in the fields, and on the heaths. Carl's father wished him to be a preacher, too, when he grew up—he could think of nothing better in all God's world. But little Carl's early rambles looking for flowers decided his life for him—he wanted to be a naturalist.

First, he had to earn some money before he could begin his studies, so he was apprenticed to a shoemaker. But few flowers bloomed about the poor shoemaker's door. Fortunately, Carl's schoolmaster knew his love of flowers, and he helped him all he could. In time, he found his way up to the great University of Lund.

Carl's father could only let him have eight pounds a year, so he had to manage with very small meals, and few clothes; and he had to mend his shoes with thick paper and the bark of trees. But he was so eager, that a doctor, who had a lot of books, gave him the free run of his library. Despite his poverty, he gained a royal scholarship to go up to the famous University of Uppsala. There a professor set him to the task of describing all the plants and flowers mentioned in the Bible. Carl liked that. In time he knew enough to take pupils himself.

When he was twenty-four years old, he went off exploring to Lapland, a part of the world that people knew little of then. For some of the way he had a horse; but most of the way he had to walk with a couple of

Laplanders to keep him company. In the end, he found a hundred unknown plants; and on his return, the professors of the University were so pleased with him that they gave him ten pounds, the cost of his journey. But the new flowers were Carl's best reward.

Next he found himself in Holland in the employ of a clever banker with a wonderful garden. To young Carl Linné it was paradise. Each day, he rose at dawn; each night, he continued his studies long after dark. It was then that he began to write of the beautiful things he had found, so that others might enjoy them.

In time, he set himself an even bigger task—not only to collect flowers and to name them—but to list the various species in order. This had never been properly done before; some of the names by which the flowers were known were many words long, descriptions rather than names. He was clever at Latin, which was a happy thing, so he was able to reduce the long clumsy names to short exact ones. Latin was already known round the world.

Carl Linné's work earned him fame. Just as he exchanged the long clumsy flower descriptions for short neat Latin names, those who wished to honour him, changed his own name into a nice-sounding Latin one— so that all round the world today he is known as *Linnaeus* —Carl Linnaeus.

Once, he paid a visit to England, looking for rare plants and flowers, because he never lost his love of them. And when he saw the golden glory of the gorse blooming on Putney Heath, he fell down on his knees at once to thank God for its beauty. Another time, when he came upon a little wild flower growing in an unexpected place, he cried out with joyous wonder: 'God has been here!'

Carl was not called by God to be a preacher, but everywhere he went, he helped people to know that God is behind all the beauty and wonder of the earth, and to give thanks.

E

Joe, the Clown

How would you like to be a clown? Perhaps you would sooner be an engine-driver or a missionary. But to be a clown—a really good clown, with a pasty white forehead and a big red nose, and the power to make people laugh—is a wonderful thing.

I want to tell you about a little boy who became a clown—the most famous of all clowns. His name was Joseph Grimaldi. Little Joe was born in London. His father was an Italian actor, seventy years old when his little boy was born. He wasn't a very kind father, or a very patient one. He used to whack Joe very hard when he was still quite small. He wanted him to be a little dancer, and to act in pantomime, and whenever he failed to do as he thought he should, he whacked him.

But all the whackings in the world couldn't drive the laughter out of little Joe's heart and when he was nine and his father died, he still went on acting in pantomime and dancing. But he couldn't earn his living by that alone, and he had to work in his uncle's butcher-shop as well. He didn't much like counting out the sausages and chopping up the joints—he wanted to be not a butcher, but a clown.

And he did become a clown, the most famous clown in all England. People came from far and near to see him and hear him and laugh with him. He had many troubles of his own; his young wife died, and his own health gave way, so that he was a cripple by the time he was forty-five. But he never let the laughter die out of his heart, and he was such a wonderful clown that other people who had troubles came to love him, and went about their lives more bravely because of him.

If you go to Holy Trinity Church, Dalston, in the East End of London today, you will see a memorial to Joseph Grimaldi, the most loved of all the clowns. That is fitting, because Holy Trinity has been the official clowns' church since December 1959. It was dedicated as such by the Bishop of Stepney at a service attended by a lot of clowns, and with a clown actually reading the lesson to the people in the church. Of course, he didn't have his pasty white forehead and his big red nose, and his wide baggy pants on that day, but still he was a clown. Even a clown has feelings and longings underneath all his fun, and he needs to hear of the love of God, told in His Book, and in His church.

Close to his memorial hangs the clown's prayer, with these words beautifully printed: 'O God, who has created us with the gift of laughter, we thank Thee for Thy servants the clowns. Grant, we beseech Thee, that as we fool for the sake of all Thy servants, we may become fools for Christ's sake, content to abandon all in Thy service.'

That prayer must be a surprise to lots of people—people who have never thought about clowns being God's servants; or have never knelt down in church, or anywhere else, to thank God for sending laughter into the world. Yet surely we should thank Him for laughter every day of our lives—laughter that is clean, and full and lively—that helps us to bear our burdens when we must, to get on with other people, and to go bravely on our way.

Forty Grains

Do you like rice-pudding? The most beautiful sight some of us have seen this week was forty grains of rice. It wasn't a rice-pudding though. Forty grains would have made a very small pudding for all the people who had come specially to look.

But we weren't disappointed—not at all. In Japan, a young man, Shujo Kawai, had found out how to make from rice something more exciting than a pudding— a gallery of pictures. There were forty of them, set out in little frames with magnifying glasses, for us to see. Each little picture was painted on one shiny grain of rice, so you can guess how tiny it was. Each was in beautiful colours—painted with a hair out of a mouse's whisker, so you can guess what a tiny paint brush that would be.

You will know too what sharp eyes and clever, steady fingers young Shujo Kawai has when I tell you that he paints his beautiful little pictures without magnifying glasses of any kind.

On one of the grains of rice that he had sent from Japan to New Zealand for us to see, he had actually painted all twenty-six letters of the alphabet—ABC, all the way down to Z. Imagine it!

It must have been an exciting day when young Shujo Kawai first found out that he could do this. He was sitting at his desk, one day in 1956, when two grains of rice dropped from a bag he had brought back from the country. He picked up the grains, so very tiny, and white, and held them for a moment.

As he looked at them, a thought struck him. 'I wonder

if I could write some letters on them?' He tried—his
first effort wasn't very successful—but he kept on trying,
like every true artist. Then he tried little pictures. He
mixed his colours carefully, but until he thought of a
mouse's whisker, it was difficult to get a brush small
enough to apply his paints.

There were lots of lovely things to paint, once his
sharp eyes got used to working on such a small space, and
his steady fingers managed to grasp his brush. It took a
lot of practice, but in time, young Shujo Kawai was
painting little pictures of buildings under the blue sky,
rocky coastlines with boats bearing proud sails, gardens
in various seasons—some of the loveliest showing golden
leaves of autumn, some showing trees bowed down with
snow in winter. Each was a perfect little picture.

Gradually news of what he was doing spread, and
people came to see them. For those whose eyes were not
so sharp, little magnifying-glasses were fixed above the
pictures so that they could be enjoyed, and people came
from far and near to see them.

That gave Shujo Kawai another idea. At the time—
and still—in Japan are many poor people, suffering the
loss of their homes and all their possessions in earth-
quakes and floods. Many of them have little to eat and
to wear.

When the boys and girls in New Zealand learned this,
they joined in with their fathers and mothers to send the
Japanese people aid. They specially wanted to share
some of the good things they had, with the boys and girls.
So they took them—loads and loads and loads of them—
to the Combined Organization for the Relief of Suffering
Overseas' packing-room in New Zealand, and in time
they reached Japan.

Young Shujo Kawai was one of these poor people, and
he was so grateful, and he wondered what he could do
to say thank-you. Then he thought of his little pictures.
He picked out his very best, and then set to work to make

a special one—a beautiful little one that I saw this week. It shows a New Zealand child handing a gift to a Japanese child.

Japan is a long way across the seas from New Zealand, but when I saw that little picture of the children with their hands outstretched toward each other, I knew they had found a way to bridge the distance, and I was very glad. For I knew that in my own land were some children who had not forgotten Jesus's lovely words: *'Freely ye have received, freely give'* (Matthew 10[8]).

Richard in the Rain

ONCE long ago there was a wild stormy night. As the wind and rain sent people hurrying to their warm homes, a boy hungry and penniless, with no home to go to, curled up on a doorstep like a little puppy, to keep himself warm. His name was Richard Watts. How long he stayed curled up there nobody knows, but to him in his misery one hour seemed like six.

Then something happened that changed the whole world for Richard, and for hundreds and thousands of others. The man of the house chanced to open his front door, and to his surprise, discovered a rain-soaked bundle on his step. Was it a puppy? No! It was a boy—it was Richard. By the glint of light from his open door, the good man stooped down to him, and with a word, brought him inside.

First of all the good man had to find him some clothes, because he was soaked. He hadn't anything to fit exactly, and Richard looked a funny little sketch, but that didn't matter—he was out of the rain.

Then the good man did a lovely thing that has never been forgotten. We don't know his name—just as we don't know the name of the Good Samaritan. After he had taken Richard in and clothed him he set a meal before him; and in the morning, when it was time for him to go on his way again, he sent him off with fourpence in his pocket.

It might not seem much, but to Richard it was the changing of his fortune. He kept part of his fourpence, and with courage born of the kindness of the good man, set out to earn; more than that, there was born in his

own heart a desire to do for others who might need it
some kind deed like the good man had done for him, if
he ever got the chance. His hard work brought results
and in time he became a very rich man with land and
houses in the lovely county of Kent.

One of the nicest things he did when he grew up, was
to have built in the High Street of Rochester, a house
with a fine, sturdy roof that would keep out the rain, and
a door that would open whenever there was need, to
six poor travellers. They were as welcome as he had been
in the good man's house. And to make sure it would go
on as long as there was need, he wrote down his wish
simply and plainly, so that everybody would understand
it. 'Every Poor Traveller admitted to the house,' his
writing said, 'shall have a lodging for the night in a room
by himself. The Trustees (that is, the people who were
to keep the house open, ready and warm) shall cause a
supper to be provided in the Common Room every eve-
ning at 7 o'clock, for the Poor Travellers. Each Poor
Traveller', it said, 'shall depart from the house by
10 o'clock in the morning, and shall on his departure
receive from the Master *the sum of four-pence*. Each Traveller's food allowance', he said, 'shall consist of half a
pound of meat, a pound of bread, and a pint of coffee,
and a pint of coffee in the morning.'

Richard did this lovely thing because he remembered
how the good man had treated him, and you can still
visit in the High Street of Rochester the house that
Richard built.

It was just the sort of thing Jesus had in mind when
He said: '*All things whatsoever ye would that men should do
to you, do ye even so to them*' (Matthew 7[12]).

The Potato Crisp Man

Not long ago there lived in London a boy called Frank Smith—quite an ordinary sort of name, and to some he must have seemed an ordinary boy.

He belonged to a big family of seven children, and his father was a greengrocer. Often when he went to Covent Garden Market to buy cabbages, he used to take Frank with him. Frank liked that, for there were lots of things to see, and lots of people who, like his father, came to buy produce for their shops. Soon, the great piles of greens, and crates of fruit, and sacks of potatoes were loaded on to carts and lorries for all parts of London.

When it was time for Frank to leave school, he began to think seriously about what he would do in the world. He remembered his trips to the market, and he remembered seeing his mother make dishes of potato crisps for her big family. And he thought to himself: 'That would be a nice thing to be. I will be a potato crisp man!'

Without losing any time, he started. He washed his potatoes, peeled and sliced them thinly and cooked them as he had many a time watched his mother do hers. Then he popped them into neat little paper-bags to be sold at a penny each.

In the next weeks he found a good many customers, but he needed to sell many thousands of penny bags to make much of a living. First of all he had to spend quite a bit of money in buying his potatoes, and pay for the fuel to cook them. He called them 'Smith's Crisps' and nowadays they are known by everybody in England. I will tell you why.

One day, thinking how he could sell more, Frank hit upon a wonderful idea. He got a lot of little pieces of blue paper and into each he put a pinch of salt. Then screwing them up, he popped one into each bag of crisps. That made all the difference. Frank's customers shook the little blue packets of salt over their crisps, and found them good. In a little while they were back for more, and others whom they told of their find came too.

In time, Frank bought farmlands to grow his own potatoes, for he was beginning to need so many. Soon he was selling not hundreds and thousands, but millions and millions.

The salt made all the difference.

Nowadays, salt is cheap—we call it common salt; but it wasn't always so. Once it was so precious that it was offered to the gods, and there were wars waged to get possession of salt-springs; soldiers were paid often, not in money, but in salt—hence our word *salary*, which comes from an ancient word, *salarium*, meaning soldier's salt-money. A bag of salt was reckoned as precious as a man's life. There are still places in the world, travellers tell us, where men will sell their wives and children for salt; and there are places where children—believe it or not—would sooner have a lump of salt than a lump of sugar. It is precious because it makes such a difference.

Jesus talked about salt. Those who listened to Him understood His meaning at once, because in the crowd were fishermen like Peter and Andrew. Salt was an everyday need of theirs, to *preserve* their fish, and *to bring out its flavour*.

That, as the potato crisp man discovered, is still what salt does. That is what Jesus means when He says to His friends: 'Ye are the salt of the earth'—you are those who, mingling in the affairs of every day, are keeping life good, and giving it added flavour (Matthew 5[13]). That is what He means when He says to His friends:

'*Let there be salt between you*' (Mark 9⁵⁰, Moffatt). Let your religion—your love, your thought, your joy—be like salt, keeping everything in life fresh and attractive between you.

Salt, you see, makes such a difference!

Ready for the Road

In the holidays, the boys and girls who live in Auckland love nothing so much as to go to the Zoo. They have lots of friends there—chief among them, Jamuna the elephant, patient and strong, fifty years old. She gives them exciting rides. They like that, and I think Jamuna does, too.

But just now, sad to say, there are no rides for anyone. Jamuna has sore feet. The other morning her picture was in the paper, with the heading in large letters: 'JAMUNA MAY WEAR BOOTS.'

Now this, of course, is not as simple as it sounds. Jamuna can't go into a shop and get fitted as you can, and come out with a parcel under her arm. If she is really to have boots, she will have to have them made specially.

Meanwhile, she is bathing her sore feet in a solution of Epsom salts. The elephant walk at the Zoo is to be sealed, and made a bit smoother. Having sore feet is no joke to Jamuna; nor, indeed, to the boys and girls who are missing their rides.

'An elephant in boots' sounds as funny as a 'puss in boots' or 'a goose in shoes'.

One day Mr Flick left his little farm to drive a flock of geese into town to market and upon each goose he put a pair of shoes. You wonder how he managed it?

Well, first he drove them into a specially prepared pen with melted tar on the ground. When the geese had walked on the tar, and got their feet all black and tacky, he drove them into another place with fine sand all over the ground. You can guess what happened. The fine sand stuck, and in no time Mr Flick's geese all had shoes.

They must have looked funny—as funny as Jamuna in boots. But their feet were at least saved from becoming sore on the hard roads, and that, as Jamuna and the silliest goose knows—is what boots and shoes are for.

When the world was young nobody wore them, but soon they found the need and got busy making them. Some were of wood, some of leather, some of cloth; some were ornamented with jewels, some lined with gold, some even bound with iron and brass.

Roads in those days were very difficult, with holes, and thorns, and cracked stones that cut the feet. So everybody who had to travel long distances saw to it that his feet were well shod.

Some of the most important of these were messengers: 'How beautiful upon the mountains', says the Bible, 'are the feet of him that bringeth good tidings, that publisheth peace, that bringeth good tidings of good, that publisheth salvation; that saith . . . Thy God reigneth!' (Isaiah 52[7]).

The messengers, you may be sure, were well shod; their message was so important. And when Paul came to write to his friends among the early Christians, he remembered them, and copied into his letter those words: 'How beautiful are the feet of them that preach the gospel of peace, and bring glad tidings of good things!' (Romans 10[15]). In another letter, he wrote: '*Have your feet shod*' (Ephesians 6[15], Moffatt). He was thinking not only of the messengers—preachers and missionaries and teachers, today—but of us all, even boys and girls. To him, being well shod is a sign of *readiness to go* anywhere, over rough or smooth, to take to others the good news of the Gospel.

An Exciting Find

HAVE you ever looked out of your window, and seen the world carpeted in white? What fun it is then to wrap up well and go out snowballing! Cold toes and chilled fingers are forgotten and cheeks are soon rosy. The tiny feathery snowflakes that have fallen while we have been asleep, pressed together with gloved hands, are just the thing for a battle royal.

But have you ever looked at a snow-flake all by itself? There is an interesting question in the Bible which asks: '*Hast thou entered into the treasures of the snow?*' (Job 38²²).

Next time, while snow is still falling, take out a piece of black cardboard or cloth and catch some of the tiny flakes. They will show up well against that background. If you can, look at the shape of the snowflakes under a microscope.

On a quiet farm in Vermont in America, there once lived a boy called Wilson Bentley who loved the snow. He loved the fun of it—the snowballing, the tobogganing, and the building of a snow-man, with an old hat stuck on his head at a jaunty angle, two pebbles for his eyes, a stick for his nose, and a red carrot stuck in for his mouth.

But most of all, Wilson loved the beauty of the snowflakes. When he was ten, he asked his family if they could buy him a camera so that he could photograph them.

Now this was a daring request, because they weren't very rich and they knew that a camera good enough to photograph small beautiful things like snowflakes would have to be a very good camera indeed. They talked about it for a long time; they had never heard of anyone photographing snowflakes. But little Wilson Bentley was so keen that at last they clubbed together and found the money to buy him the camera he wanted.

Then a wonderful thing happened: Wilson had not been taking photographs long when he made an exciting discovery—*that every single snowflake was different*. So he found himself, as the Bible says, 'entering into the treasures of the snow'. His camera was properly fitted with equipment to enlarge each tiny snowflake, so that he was able to get a really good look at it. Imagine it!

All his life Wilson Bentley lived on that farm, and winter by winter he used that same camera, till by the end of his life he had photographed four hundred thousand snowflakes! Each had to be handled with the greatest possible patience and care.

He never became rich, but what he learned of 'the treasures of the snow' gave him hours and hours of joy. Scientists all over the world studied his beautiful pictures and were excited about them. For a long time some of them had wondered about the shape of snowflakes, but now Wilson could show them beyond doubt that each is different. The tiny, dry, feathery particles begin life up in the sky as crystals of clear ice fastened to each other. So tiny, so fragile, so easily melted, each snowflake reflects the light as it comes down, and looks to our eyes beautifully white. Some have six sides, and look like little stars, some are like tiny flowers, some are like jewels —and every single one of the thousands and millions and billions that fall is different! Isn't that a breath-taking thought?

If we had been making snowflakes enough to cover the ground in wintertime, I think we might have been satisfied to settle on one good pattern. But God isn't like that —He loves to make beautiful things, and to take infinite care in the making of them. In all the world there are no two snowflakes exactly alike; and what is even more wonderful, there are no two boys, or two girls exactly alike. God makes each person lovingly: He cares for what He makes. *He cares for you!* (1 Peter 5⁷).

James's Choice

WHEN James Naismith was as old as you, he had no idea what he was going to do in the world and neither had anybody else.

He grew up on a farm in Ontario, where there were plenty of interesting things to do. He learned to drive horses, and to saw logs that smelt nice as the saw bit into them and the sawdust fell out, to feed the animals about the farm, and to fish, and hunt. But if Jimmie thought of being a farmer, it wasn't for long.

When he was old enough, he entered McGill University—a very famous university in Montreal. It was very different from being on the farm, but James soon settled down. He enjoyed his studies, and got on so well that when the time came to leave he had earned eleven passes. One of them was for music, and some people, knowing how he loved it, thought that he might give his life to music, but that was not his choice.

From McGill University, where he had been so happy and successful, he moved to a big college where young men went to be trained as ministers, the Presbyterian Theological Seminary. But he didn't mean to be a minister—not the usual kind of minister who preaches, and teaches, and visits the sick, and gets to know his people.

Young James Naismith chose to do something quite unusual. A fine, lively Christian, it happened that he was very good at games, and it seemed to him that he could do a lot to make the world a happier and better place, if he could teach boys and girls, and men and women to play games eagerly and well.

When the time came, he crossed over from his country

into America, and began to help boys and men play games at the Y.M.C.A.

Soon he noticed a curious thing—that there was no good team game to play between the end of the football season and the beginning of the baseball season. So he set about inventing one. It was such a good game, that soon the boys and men were no longer allowed to keep it to themselves. The girls and young women wanted to play it, too. Now we all play it. I wonder if you know the game?

James Naismith got a lot of fun out of making it up— and a lot of fun out of playing it. First, he set up a pole at each end of the field—two big poles each ten feet high—and then he nailed an empty peach-basket to the top of each.

The game took on; everybody in the place wanted to play, and nearly everybody did—at times there were as many as fifty players on each side! It must have been a dangerous scramble, and the poor referee must have had a hopeless job.

You know what the game is, of course—it's basketball, and this is how it started. Now young people play it all round the world.

When James Naismith died in November 1939 he was still a Presbyterian minister, by rights, but he had spent all the forty years of his busy working life, teaching people to play well. The world in which God set him is a happier, better place because of it.

You see, there are so many different ways of helping God and His people. It has always been that way. When the first people gathered in the Church, Paul said: 'He granted some men to be apostles, some to be prophets, some to be evangelists, some to shepherd and teach' (Ephesians 4[11], Moffatt). Since then, He has set men and women to do other tasks as well. Though, of course, there is only one secret—it's in the New Testament: '*Whatsoever you do, let it be done for the glory of God*' (1 Corinthians 10[31], Moffatt).

The Years Will Tell

LITTLE Alexander Fleming lived at Lochfield Farm, in a lonely part of Scotland. But he was never lonely. There were so many things to do. Great winds kept the air sweet and clean in that high place, waving playful patterns in the grass. Alexander and his brothers and sisters loved to play there, and when school was done to come to their home surrounded by sheltering trees. There were eight of them and Alexander was the youngest.

When he was five years old—two years before his father died—he went to school. It was a 'wee school in the country away beyond Darvel'. That is how he always remembered it—a stone cottage, with only two rooms and about thirteen pupils. 'But that wee school up on the hill,' he used to say, 'that's where they really taught you something.' The name of Alexander's first teacher was Miss Marion Stirling. He never forgot her, and she never forgot him. Years and years later, when all the world was echoing with his name, she wrote him a letter, and glad and proud he was to get it.

When Alexander was not at school, or helping about the farm he loved to go for long tramps up on the hills around Lochfield. He loved the wind playing games in the grass; in places there was purple heather in the late summer and early autumn; when the snows of winter came, some of the high hills put on white caps. In the spring everything became green again, and the busy little streams on their way down to the Glen Water ran sparkling in the sun.

Alexander was always thinking up things to do—a new way to trap rabbits, a good way to tickle trout, a place to find peewits' eggs. Sometimes with an elder brother he roamed the high places with their dog to be sure that no stray sheep got into trouble. But tickling trout —catching them by hand—was his favourite fun. It took a lot of patience, and sharp eyes, and steady hands. But he often had a little string of trout for the family breakfast, and very sweet they were. Alexander never forgot those happy times.

Soon he moved to another school four miles away, and it meant a long walk there and back; and soon he went on to the Academy and harder studies. That meant staying away from home during the week, and coming home at week-ends, part of the distance by train, and the rest on foot. But he did it cheerfully and said it helped to keep him fit. All his life he did everything he could to keep his body strong and well—he had such important work to do in the world. He was very modest about it, but the world is a different place today because of young Alexander Fleming.

By the time he was ready to work, his brother Thomas who had gone to London, and become a doctor of eyes, invited him to come down. Robert and John, the two brothers nearest him in age, had already joined brother Thomas, and were studying to become spectacle-makers.

At first, Alexander, who was still only fourteen, didn't quite know what he wanted to be. Noting his quick brain and clear eyes and steady, patient hands, Thomas said: 'Why don't you train to be a doctor?'

He thought it over, and it seemed to him a good idea. With the help of brother Thomas, he chose St Mary's Hospital, Paddington, as the place where he would train. It meant hard work, but he loved it. 'If you ask me how to be successful,' he said, years later when everybody wanted to know his secret, 'I would say—work, work, and work again.' But that was only part of his secret. He loved helping sick people to get well.

For a long time in his room at the hospital he had been

studying the microbes that caused diseases, and trying to find something to kill them, and make people better. It took a lot of thought and hard work and patience. So he was very glad when something too small for the eye to see, blew in at his window. Then one day he noticed that the little invisible thing that had blown in on to where he was working with his microscope had grown into blue mould something like that on an old piece of cheese. He put a tiny piece of the mould on to some broth and watched it grow bigger. All his time was now given to studying the mould, and sick people all round the world are grateful that he did, for that was how he discovered penicillin, one of the world's great healing substances.

It was exciting, but it took years and years before it could be prepared in large quantities and in a form that doctors could use. Alexander Fleming wrote articles and gave lectures to help others to understand it, and with the help of other clever doctors and chemists the thing was done. Penicillin was tried out on white mice, then on rabbits, then on men and women—and it did wonderful things. All the world rose up to thank God for penicillin —and for Alexander Fleming. One doctor who worked with him, when he saw what penicillin could do, said: 'It looks like a miracle!' It was—and it is—the healing of God coming to sick men and women and little children all over the world, through the patient discovery of Alexander Fleming.

God is always looking for boys and girls to help Him to make the world a better place. The minister and the people who have put in their church near the hospital a lovely stained-glass window of Alexander Fleming working, hope that those who see it will remember that. Certainly, I remembered it, when I walked into that lovely church a little while ago; and now I have told you this wonderful story, so that you can begin to consider what it is that God has for you to do.

The Lazy Barnacle

THERE came to a port in Australia the other day a wonderful new ship—the *City of Sydney*. She was on her maiden voyage, her very first trip out into the great seas of the world.

And there was something else about her that was very interesting to the boys and girls who gathered to see her. She hadn't any barnacles. You know what barnacles are, of course; you have seen them on old boats upturned on the beach when you have been swimming in the holidays, or on rocks when you have been poking about on the shore. The ones you have seen, of course, were dead, because barnacles can't live where the water does not wash over them.

They are funny little things, with their shells glued tightly to the rocks. It is impossible to get them off without easing them with something very strong and sharp—and then they nearly always break. So sharp are their broken shells that they can cut like knives.

They are the special enemy of ships. They love to fasten themselves on the hull of a ship below the waterline, and when a lot of them have done so, they interfere with the ship's progress. Then she has to go into dock and have them scraped off.

But those who have built the big new ship, *City of Sydney*, have found a new way to deal with the barnacles. Instead of waiting to have them scraped off—and it is a hard, tedious job—she has a regular wash from the ship's bilge keels and keel plates below the waterline. The mixture is something less agreeable than warm, soapy water, for it is poisonous. But at the proper time

St. Paul's Methodist Church, Shaw

invite you to their

CHRISTMAS FAYRE

on

Saturday, 1st December 1979
to be opened at 3.00 p.m.
by Mr. & Mrs. H. WARD

Admission: Adults 20p
               Children 10p

Proceeds for Church Funds
(Please pay at entrance)

OPENING CEREMONY

3.00 p.m. Welcome

HYMN

While shepherds watched their flo[
All seated on the ground, (by ni[
The angel of the Lord came down,
And glory shone around.

Fear not, said he; for mighty drea[
Had seized their troubled mind:
Glad tidings of great joy I bring
To you and all mankind.

To you, in David's town, this day
Is born, of David's line,
A Saviour, who is Christ the Lord
And this shall be the sign:

The heavenly Babe you there shall
To human view displayed,   (f[
All meanly wrapped in swaddling b[
And in a manger laid.

All glory be to God on high,
And to the earth be peace;
Good will henceforth from heaven t
Begin and never cease.   (me[

PRAYER

CHAIRMAN'S ADDRESS

MUSICAL ITEMS - Junior Dept.

ANNOUNCEMENTS

THANKS

OPENING

STALLS

Gifts,   Produce,   Bric-a-Brac,
Fancy goods,   Bottle,
Cakes,   'Florin'

Father Christmas

Minerals,   Ice Creams
Sweets

TEAS at 4.00 p.m. and 4.45 p.m.
(Tickets on sale after Opening)

EVENING ENTERTAINMENT

5.30 p.m. Film "Shipwreck"

7.30 p.m. Oldham Banjo, Guitar
& Mandoline Band

8.30 p.m.   Supper

9.00 p.m. Oldham Banjo, Guitar
& Mandoline Band

OTHER CHRISTMAS ARRANGEMENTS

Sunday 2nd December at 10.30 a.m.
Gift Service

Saturday 8th December at 7.30 p.m.
Carol Concert

Sunday 16th December at 7.30 p.m.
Film "Force 10 from Navarone"

Sunday 23rd December

Morning service 10.30 a.m.
Carols by Candlelight 6.00 p.m.

Monday 24th December at 7.00 p.m.

Christmas Eve Social

Christmas Day

11.00 a.m. Service, to which
Boys and Girls are invited to
bring their toys.

Saturday 29th December to 5th Jan.

Family Pantomime
"Land of Dreams"

TEA TICKETS

it slowly rises up the ship to the water-line, and slowly kills all the unwelcome barnacles, which is a very good saving of time and trouble.

Now I must tell you something very curious about these barnacles. Most people think, because of their hardness, that they are related to limpets, oysters and clams. But that isn't true. Actually, they are distant cousins of crabs and prawns, very soft little things of the sea. The little legs which they thrust out of the top of their shells are as soft as a tiny curled feather, and they keep them out all the time to kick into their hungry mouths the food they need.

I wonder if you have ever heard the saying, 'As lazy as a barnacle'? Now why has the barnacle come to be a byword for laziness? Well, it begins its life, of course, in a very different way from that in which it ends it, clamped to a rock or the hull of a great ship. At first the barnacle has tiny eyes, three pairs of hairy legs, a tail, and a piece of shell armour like the crab wears. He can swim well, and get about in the sea and catch what he wants to eat. He is really a very active fellow.

But after a while a change comes over him. He gets tired of looking for food, and too lazy to swim about. He finds what he thinks is a good place, settles down, and grows a hard shell over himself. After that, he never moves again as long as he lives. Now he has to wait till the food comes to him. In time, his eyes and legs and tail disappear; and if he gets left above high-water mark, he dies.

That is the sad story of the barnacle—*what he doesn't use, he loses*. And do you know, boys and girls are a bit like barnacles. God has given us wonderful powers— powers of seeing and hearing and feeling, powers of praying and worshipping, and powers of helping people, being unselfish, and entering fully into life. But if we don't use those powers, we lose them, just like the lazy barnacle. We have to love and think and worship and help if we want to be fully alive.

Good-bye to a Friend

NOT even the Queen could save the friendly little farthing, though the bells of the City churches still ring out over the London she loves:

'Oranges and lemons', say the bells of St Clement's;
'You owe me five farthings', say the bells of St Martin's.

She could not save it although she still treasures the golden coach in which she rode five miles through London's cheering millions on one unforgettable day. That coach, with its carved figures and scrolls and panel-paintings and gold, cost—what do you think? Of course, you'd never guess: £7,587 19s. 9d., and two farthings!

The farthing has 'outlived its usefulness'. That is what Mr Barker, one of the Queen's men, said; and the Queen made a proclamation that after the close of the year 1960 the farthing could no longer be used.

For four years before the time was up, no more were minted, though some seven hundred and fifty millions of them are still somewhere around in corners of pockets and purses and in children's money-boxes. The truth is, I expect, people are sorry to part with the tiny coin with its Jenny wren on one side; and they have tried to keep at least one of them—though it's no use any more.

There was a time when it could buy a lot, as father and mother, and especially grandfather and grandmother can tell—a tiny book, a pencil, a whip-top, a twist of sweets large enough to last quite a long time. There was actually a Farthing Shop in Clerkenwell, London, where wonderful things could be had. But that has all gone—

and now the little farthing has gone, too. They say it has 'outlived its usefulness'.

It had a long, long, life, of course. It began with the Anglo-Saxon silver penny, deeply impressed with a cross so that it could be broken into four equal parts called *fourthlings*. That is how the little coin got its name. After that, about seven hundred years ago, separate farthings were made; they were silver, too.

Then changes came. For about three hundred years the little coin was made of copper. Then for a while it was changed to tin. Two hundred years nearer our own time it was decided to melt the tin and copper together, and make it of bronze.

Now it has gone altogether. I shouldn't be surprised if the Queen was a little sad to have to make that proclamation about the passing of the farthing. But what could she do? The little coin has 'outlived its usefulness', though it has stayed with men and women and boys and girls for seven hundred years.

Thank goodness, *there are some things which last for ever*. Do you know what they are? Turn to the ending of one of the favourite passages in the Bible and you will find out—1 Corinthians 13[13], R.V. 'Now', it says, 'abideth faith, hope and love, these three; but the greatest of these is love.'

Old Pete the Trapper

WHAT would you do if you suddenly met a great grizzly bear in the woods, or came home and found one in your bed? What would you do if you had to drive a dog-team through deep snow, or set a trap to catch a wolf?

These are the sort of adventures Evelyn Berglund and her two sisters had in their everyday life, up in the Arctic Circle. They lived in a little wood cabin, but a big part of the year they were miles and miles from it. For they were trappers.

It was a hard life, especially when Father Berglund fell ill. Every now and again he had to go into hospital; and even when he came home, there were lots of things he couldn't do, he was so crippled. Then he died. The girls were only ten, twelve and thirteen, and with their mother they just had to carry on. Their living was to trap wild animals for furs, and their trapline ran two hundred and eighty miles beyond Fort Yukon. That is a long, long way, and there were no neighbours, or roads.

In the next twelve years they got to know all about musk-rats, and bears and moose; they learned to shoot straight, and to fish for salmon in the great rivers. They needed to do both, or they would have starved, for there were no shops to go to. Besides, there were their healthy, hungry dogs, that when the countryside was covered with deep snow pulled their sledges. Sometimes they went berry-picking; sometimes they watched the beavers in the river; weeks and weeks were taken up with chopping and piling wood, or in making clothes, mitts, shoes and caps out of dried skins.

Always, in the coldest time, the animal traps stretching

over miles and miles had to be minded; and when the
wild animals had been caught, they had still to be piled
on the sledge and got home.

It was a hard life, but neither Evelyn—who wrote a
book about their adventures—nor her two sisters, Hazel
and Elsie, felt sorry for themselves. They hadn't time for
that; and there were so many things to learn about.
Sometimes Indians, hunting in the woods, came to their
cabin.

Pete Nelson and John Roberts and Bill O'Brien were
all trappers, and when the summer came after Father
Berglund died, they joined to go upriver with Mrs
Berglund and the girls to help them. Pete was an old man,
slender and strong and friendly. He had a little house of
his own away up the river, and he was always eager to
get there. But it was a long way and the river was tricky,
and though ten days ought to have brought them to it,
the difficulties with the big clumsy boats, with twenty-
five restless dogs and all the gear and all the food packed
on them, were so great that it took about sixty days.
There were lots of camps to be made, wet or fine, and
lots of dangers to be met.

You can guess, then, how happy everybody was, and
how really excited old Pete was, when they got to his
place at last. Evelyn tells about it. 'There's my house!'
he cried with joy. 'Thank God for my house!'

Then they started unloading. It looked like rain, and
the girls helped old Pete to carry his things up lest they
should all get wet. 'Here, take the beans,' he said to
Elsie, as he handed them over. 'Thank God for the
beans.' And every time he handed up something to
carry up the bank to his little house, he thanked God for
it. 'Here, take a sack of flour. Thank God for the
flour. Case of corn. Thank God for the corn. Sugar.
Thank God for the sugar.' And suddenly, as Hazel
picked up a bag, old Pete, out of his heart, cried: 'Thank
God for Hazel!'

He sounds a very nice old man, doesn't he? We don't know much about him, but we know this one important thing: he had a thankful heart for all the common ordinary things of life. St Paul spoke of '*giving thanks always for all things unto God*' (Ephesians 5[20]), and that was old Pete's secret. No wonder everybody liked him. It's a secret you could copy.